FINISHING LINE PRESS
www.finishinglinepress.com

I0835421

ONCE READ AS RUIN

New Women's Voices Series, No. 163

poems by

Katherine Gaffney

Finishing Line Press
Georgetown, Kentucky

ONCE READ AS RUIN

New Women's Voices Series, No. 163

For Michael Madonick,
without whom this chapbook would not have been possible.
Thank you for the lunches at the house by the sea
where we inevitably talked poetry.

ISBN 978-1-64662-699-1 First Edition

ACKNOWLEDGMENTS

"The Call," *jubilat*
"Once Read as Ruin," *Rabbit Catastrophe*
"In April," *Kettle Blue Review*
"Hole in the Barn Door Quilt," *Meridian*
"Matroneum," *Storyscape Literary Journal*

Thank you to Dylan Loring for being the finest of editors.

Publisher: Leah Huete de Maines
Editor: Christen Kincaid
Cover Art: Manuel G. Runyan
Author Photo: Kyle Stevens
Cover Design: Elizabeth Maines McCleavy

Order online: www.finishinglinepress.com
also available on amazon.com

Author inquiries and mail orders:
Finishing Line Press
PO Box 1626
Georgetown, Kentucky 40324
USA

Table of Contents

LIKE A SALMON (OR FOOL IN A BLUE HOUSE)

I feel like a fool in a blue house, thought I could curate
the life we'd live—repot herbs in spring, summer dinners
on the deck, year-round sex on the couch. Saturday
we'd bake bread. Sunday we'd walk in the sleepy
evening steadying ourselves for the week. But we've got
none of that, except for sex on the couch. He's bought
in, even with the front door open, weather permitting,
where extra quiet becomes a game we play. He says
his grandmother, in old age, was like a salmon,
wanting to return to Czechoslovakia, "fuck, then die."
"Fuck, then die," is a thought I've had in our bed —
how a woman in a too-large oxford shirt communicates
sex, for me, translates to never getting off
my my-size shirt. Please excuse the post-it notes,
it's just the dishes are dry and could stand to be re-homed
or the mail has piled up again on the counter and I can't find
the surface. Perhaps it would be easier to write in a chorus.
I've gone about this all wrong—this is not chess or a set
of stringy marionettes where, if I leave the pieces for a day,
I can return to them unmoved.

I.

Marriage is not

a house or even a tent
it is before that, and colder.

—Margaret Atwood

AT LONGHORN STEAKHOUSE

I can't see how we sit in any romance. Sticky booth, fake
bull horns divert indefinable energy that should course

across a table of lovers or potential lovers or blow the table
to smithereens so we're left with a pile of rubble to make a mess

of ourselves on. I'm in love but I don't like the frame we're in.
I want to bring it to the local framing shop and pick out

something gaudy and golden. I want our photos black and white
for the printer's added pink to our cheeks as though we're fresh

flush off a mattress or off the smithereened table that is still
unrepaired in the Longhorn Steakhouse; where instead they

screwed in a plaque above the booth *Here lay a young couple in love,*
may this destruction be proof of the power of love. I am so concerned

with showmanship—an orchid on an office desk, a rock on a ring
finger. In this age of audience I want to find the boxing

ring where my grandparents called each other *Yankee* and *Rebel*
in South Dakota—a crowd screaming for boxer's blood.

SWALLOWING BLUE

We're hooked on a show that tours us
through excessively excessive homes.
One, monstrous and a garish white,
is modeled after yachts with Gucci black

lacquer walls and a gold encrusted
abstraction of a city skyline. Another
has a room for one woman's three
-hundred shoes and two kitchens,

in case she bores of the other. We fell
in love with the house with a maze
and a pavilion yoga studio. We play
the lottery. Watch each week for

the little white globes to bubble over,
wait for the numbers to match ours.
If only we could win. We'd find a plot
of land sandy and fresh, construct

our own with excesses right for us.
Maybe a maze, one kitchen, sea salt
eating at the cushions on the wrap
-around porch so each year I'd have

to find a new affordable set to make
the reedy wicker sittable again. I know
he'd like a large house in a small town.
I see the clever game of scale, but I

want a cottage before a big sea—blue
swallowing the house smaller. His scale
in reverse. How easily we forget our size
as we mill about behind paned windows.

Or how easily we inflate
our size as we pass through archways
proportioned for our heights. How we
sit before the shrunken humans framed

behind the television screen as they stumble
through and by halls and walls built to fit us
our movements, happiness. The sea cares not.
Swallows snow as if the snow never existed

to fall in the first place, homes who mock
its body from the shore. Sweet swelling, you,
who taunts the houses closer, for the moon's
reflection, for the heat that shepherds storms

to doorsteps. I will the danger, to feel small
and swallowed, but you see when I hear
the sea, I sleep. Whereas the sound tells him
to run, run from a hurricane. And as he wakes,

wet and salty, I think, *ah, the sea come in,*
but know the correct answer is sweat.
That the wet cotton pool beneath him
in bed is not the sea coming through

his body but his body ridding himself
of the sea's stress. He tells me of an old
family map—a slice of an island that once
bore his name or a name that is his through

genealogy. He awes at what it would be like
to have this land, with the portion cut out,
reserved for sheep to graze, but not cattle
or horses. To think of only sheep grazing

on grass we own and I want to say we
could have the whole sea before us, no
fences to build and millions of fish nibbling
away at algae deep below and we would not

be able to name them nor mourn them
if they were slaughtered, as the sheep might be
for Frenched lamb. But he thinks of the wool,
and of me and the yarn I could spin, natural

and creamy. How can I argue at my place
in this fantasy as we run ourselves through
the maze, in our minds, laughing too loud
in hopes we could find each other.

How breathless we are from our sofa,
a concoction of love and dream, drawing
the air out of our lungs like pearls
plucked from a tired oyster's tongue.

MATRONEUM

Architectonic. Stop. This space
matronly, once, ought not be
reduced vestigial, to a thrust. Let's write,
the Myth of or Mystery at or make
whispers of fairies, ghostly dresses
singing from their once posts, turning
once into ever after. Let's think:

ALL THE DEAR BEASTIES

A snail can sleep for three years and cows can sleep
standing up, but lie down to dream as I lie down
restless, wanting everything and sleep. I can hear
the snails slurp back into their shells and cows' great

weight compact the crinkling hay, bedding their night
-cooled stalls. My mother calls this *my mom ears*
growing in, sensitivity to the slightest creaks,
anticipating the patter of feet, my body wants me

to produce, who might seek out a glass of water
or a spot in my bed. But the anticipation is all body,
when my mind only wants sleep. Some dead guy
once said, *after sex, all animals are sad, except roosters*

and women, but I can say I am an exception and often,
not always, find myself sad after, feeling I've lost a part
like an earring or a soul. When dogs, domesticated
or wild, hear a yelp, they swarm the source of the wincing

cry to end the suffering, the weakness in the pack.
My father must have wondered whether I was
the weakness in our pack, as I sat for an hour
each night before a nebulizer and cable cartoons;

how the machine-hum helped my thick lungs filter
humid Florida air. My mother became less part
of our pack and more part of the dog's and, when
needed, their leader. How she tore the Golden

from the Shepherd's jowls over a few kibbles left
behind in a bowl. How she refused to fill the bowl
for days over the Golden's defiance. I tried to get her
to tear me off my brother, as I brushed electric eye

-shadow onto his lids, wanted her to haul me out
to the dog house, firmly exclaim *no*, leave me
there to stew. Maybe, in my fear, a part of me
would split like the tails my brother collected

with each lizard he tried to catch. Everyone would know
my fear, nod to accept the budding regrowth of my finger,
collarbone, or soul. The nub of birth, the grotesqueness
of development, my body so desperately feels I should

engage in, or so my fabled ears signal. How my father
keeps teasing, *six, six children, six babies, six grandchildren,*
but how the repetition gnaws at the joke, how laying
out his own infant christening gown pressed in preservation

plastic solidifies the stray from punch-line. Perhaps I am
part of my mother's pack, the spaniel who caught a land
crab in our yard, ate the body beneath the shell,
and rolled around in what was left, to stink less

of herself, and more like the carcass she'd conquered,
perhaps I'm trying to stink less like myself, less like
the possibility of mother and more anything but. No
more baby powder on my skin, no more baby's breath

in bouquets. I'll plant dogwood and cowslip, lamb's ear
and snail seed. I'll drive to agreed upon gas stations
in response to postings on Craigslist to collect: Zeus,
African soft-furred rats, one cat that *must go now*, budgies,

Deuce, Australian Cattle Dog (deaf), brown chickens
—a menagerie of flora and fauna. All my dear beasties
will congregate as if for a sermon given in Snow
White's soprano. Tails will wag, and tired shells

will still, and hay will crunch under a day's cud chewed.
A shield against the fable or written anew from old tales
of sleep and sex and weakness. And I can say I will be
the exception where my body will not tell me what to do.

FOUND

I have almost forgotten he lives here as we open and close
like chicory and moonflowers. Our dog scampers
like a tired wind-up toy, but she slows under the dogwood
tree yet to bloom, begins to paw as if restoring life. And sure
enough, he strides over through the excited, unmown grass,
identifies life too. A small rabbit clinging. She has not done it,
of that he is certain, but what has? He wades into the house
to pull from the roll a white trash bag. I know, so I turn
toward the neighbor's fence, cup my face as if a room
all its own. *I am trying to twist the bag to leave it airless,* he tells,
but have to snap the neck. I heard no snap, the bones so small
they didn't even warrant a mark of passing. Was he sure?
He cited the blood spatter against the white bag, opened
the garage's stuttering jaws and settled the tulip-eater beside
bags of orange peels and shrimp tails and used tissues.
He came back to the sun-warm deck, sipped his sweating
glass of wine as sweat slicked my thighs.

THE CALL

Sundays I hear church bells through
my kitchen window. Tuesdays it's
sirens. Take a tuning fork to my porcelain
sink, re-sing the note for you. Most nights
I hear my name. Call to tell you, to ask,
but you say it must have been the wind.
Each time I call I drop a whole herring
down my throat, harbor salt in my jaws'
hinges, working to equate you with salt,
or better yet summer lightning.

II.

And tame things have no immensity.

—Mina Loy

ONCE READ AS RUIN

I.

A torn open fetlock, summer, flies, a red
so real it turns to fiction. Sore, first golf
ball of growth tears to cleft. I fool myself

into seeing bone, but it's infection—fly
eggs lain in warm wet. A will past my own
body crops through my natural repulse, deals

with the horror of flies dancing in delight
over open meat. This meat I powder pink
to keep dry despite the velvet summer

mud. A candied coating to fragility. Infection
I wrap, fruitless, just as we, humans, pick
at scabs. The liftable lid to our first layer.

Small scale pain. Risk. The horse gnaws
on the bandage I swathed, buries bloodied
gauze in the muck, certain not to let it touch

the sweet alfalfa flake I threw over the fence
into her paddock. What silly pity I hold for
the wound she keeps reopening. How human

an idea to soothe sore with sweet: my child eating
ice cream with a broken leg, my grandmother eating
coffee yogurt after time and space were lost to her.

II.

"St. Ebba the Younger was Abbess of Coldingham, an abbey in the Scottish Borders… During a Viking raid on Scotland in A.D 879, St. Ebba mutilated her nose and upper lip with a razor, in the hopes of

discouraging the invaders from raping her. With her encouragement, the entire community followed suit."

—Orthodox Saints of the British Isles: Volume III

as Ebba the Younger

I gathered my flock in the chapter-house.
Chastity, chastity. The men to come,

their wants to take, one sacrifice
for another. Not far from the blood

we take to our lips at the chalice:
what communion in this detachment.

III.

The rain so thick it's a wonder the horse
hadn't swum into the fence post
that now launched from her shoulder

as if a lance, riderless, but ready.
I can't say if it was the sky's
contusion that makes me remember

her this way, but her blood was no
longer red—purple as the weathered
wood heaving with her labored breath,

as we weighed whether to pull out
the shred of board, or if it should stay
as she would lose too much. It's a wonder

she stood there on the cross ties,
mud up to her hocks, wet and quiet.
How despite the chill of a summer

storm she didn't dance away
from the hose, but let us spray
down her wait, heat, ache.

IV.

as Ebba the Younger

Chastities I sought to preserve like jams,
canned from orchards tended. From the mouth

of the Tweed to the gates of the abbey, lust
built itself a heavy load soon jettisoned

by imminent repulsion in our faces cracked
and bloodied. A new beauty spun in our house

to foil male hunger. Fury, fire, rubble, spurn
turned to ruins, our recipe written for chaotic

conservation, the buried sight of our ruined
faces, molten and won.

V.

As a young girl Wilgefortis was engaged to be wed to a pagan king… Being a devout Christian herself, Wilgefortis wished to remain pious and virginal, and she prayed to God to make her look displeasing so that the pagan king would not want to marry her… God's solution was to give her a beard.
—Medieval and Ancient Research Centre University of Sheffield

as the Father

Pretty pawn. I'd sold her hair as health, as possibility
of baby brought forth from between strong legs.

But her prayers of repulsion sang up to Him,
so He sprouted a bane of whiskers on a woman.

How she bristled. How hair once health now
became monstrosity, otherworldly, unweddable,

as she so sought. But how shortly she could carry
such multiplicity, nailed soon contradiction's crucifix.

VI.

I dip her muddied, silver tail in the bluing shampoo,
meant for greying ladies to keep shine in their hair.
As I stand at her rump, wait for the water to turn

from suds to grime, she falls asleep, tired of snaking
away from the hose's spritz. After grazing, the sun
has baked her dry. I braid her mane along her

muscled spine. I do this grooming to return the day
after to find the tail dusty again, the braid wild,
sprouted with knots and twigs.

VII.

Turned from girl unremarkable to *virgo fortis*, maiden,
unwed girl, or woman that is courageous. *Uncumber*,

Ontkommer one who avoids something, like suffering.
Or anew, *Kümmernis*, grief or anxiety. *Liberata, Librada,*

liberated. *Débarras*, riddance. How many names her beard
sprouted, senses, identities she bore in the hair grown

afresh. With the singly-shod fiddler playing her the tune
of her pious fiction, she hung a lantern, a body self-bridled.

VIII.

In all of this, I have not considered myself.
You see the saints, Ebba and Wilgefortis,
painted here as if with the horse in the distance
to illuminate the women in the foreground.

A horse can denote victory or lust, depending
on tradition. But perhaps there is both victory
and lust in this horse, in these women.
A victory over lust, as when I finish washing

the horse with each ritual of ride and bath,
I take on the horse's grime—a momentary
victory of clean. The dirt, from the ring
kicked up in canter and stride, stains me

an ashen figure, a noseless, bearded girl,
ready to float back to the world invisible.
As I stand at the pump to fill my car with gas,
as I buy a pear for the sugar to balance me

again after these fruitless rites, I am an island
of confusion. *How could this woman show*
herself in such a state, their eyes scream,
have we no standards any longer, what of taste,

decorum, propriety. But the horse tells me
with each post-wash roll in the mud, each tug
at the bandage to hide torn open tissue, not
to listen. That this exhibition is not new

or futile, but history. Long precedented
in defense of choice. The horse's roll
does not seek to defy me but stand
as example that she too can choose

her beauty or redefine it with muck and twigs,
blood and scar, as these women chose to preserve
images of themselves through path and presentation
resisted by the men who defined such value

for them no longer. Novel definition
from absence and addition of flesh and hair,
soil and sprig. That the ruin I once read
is not ruin at all, but reinvention.

As unencumbered, as rid of the weight
of expectation, the horse free from her
halter in a post-rain paddock picks
at the dressing well intended.

III.

Those cuts on my ribs are because I am trying to open gills before the flood comes.

—Samantha Hunt

HOLE IN THE BARN DOOR QUILT

A hole in the barn door means I'm at it
again. I'm letting in mice, fox kits to sleep
buried in the hay loft. You wouldn't like it,
wanting only to house animals you intend
to keep, who serve your purpose, but I find
such narrow definitions useless, for there
is a hole in almost everything useful—
how else did you get in?

FISH WIFE

It's mostly a life
of waiting and counting.
Each night I unhook
the stars, restrike them the next,
all floated matches red
before ignition—scales
the only glitter tumbling
onto my lap. To hear beauty,
I fashion earrings from his tired
hooks and bait, brightest in my shiplap
shack. He's well salted from years
of ocean spit and slap. But it all
falls away when honeyed tea hits
his belly, when he calls me
kitten, slips his hand to the soft
of my thigh. It's a ritual
of bringing him back
to land. I've taught myself
all the right knots that lasso
his waist back to his chair,
our bed, my table.
I am a denounced planet
he burns for. It sounds
bad, but it's balance.
Not so key that the winds listen
for my footfall but not so forgotten
that they sweep me up and out
like the nests of fur I brush
out the door.

IN APRIL

She must have carried
her belly around like a fish
bowl. Careful not to knock into corners,
bash the little gold body floating inside her.
Despite her care, it took her seven tries to carry
one home. Seven times she saw it float, belly up
in the bowl. Wanting to smash bowl, body,
the blow dryer on its hook. How her body
must have felt like snow
in this April.

WATER SONG

Rain blinks a code
I should know, waxes
into a wound spiced
numb with listening.
All the little words curl
in like hounds done
barking, like leaves
piled for burning,
crumbs to make clean
a table. I am to sew
my teeth, soft
and kissable, but I don't
listen. I'd rather
bleed forever, sign
my life away with
a needle, sewn shut
without possibility
for undoing, lie back
in animal-warm straw,
taken by pleasure's
eddies. There might be
a constellation of votives
to encircle me briefly,
to stave the hunger
waxing I am expected
to thunder through,
but water does not
obey as land,
and the votives stray,
pouting irregular circles,
a current currently in
change. The water carries
on and I have no choice
but to listen, consent
to its direction and song.

A SMALL WOMAN-MADE LIGHTHOUSE

I walk my widow's walk not to look
out on the sea and expect to see
him climb from the surf ragged
and torn, all effort to return to me,
but so I can announce my spidery
existence as I web my way through
my paces as to how to proceed.
Each evening I climb with a light
and to my neighbors I must look
like hope. A small woman-made light
-house directing one phantom ship,
but the light is for me to watch my hands
age each night, for the veins that spider
their way up from my palms' depths,
to watch how night floats through
sleep that escapes me, to watch how
empty this house is without him.
But empty is a treacherous word
— often a placeholder for grief,
for the missing, subtraction, but what
if I see this word as addition. For the space
I've gained in the wardrobe, for the far
fewer dishes left in the sink, for the bed
I can starfish my way through sleep
when I find it and not feel guilty for finding
him on the floor. And what if he sees
his subtraction as gain, for he has left
behind the pressures of closing the house's
shutters for storms, of holding my hand
when we walk into town. What if he lies
on another beach somewhere and knows
that all he owns is his body and that the sand
is not his and he has no desire to make
it so and the palm trees are not his and yet
they drop coconuts for him, as the rain
falls for me and I open my mouth knowing
no one will turn the corner and interrupt my joy.

THE HORSE

This horse was born from a carousel; she tore off one morning
when the man who took the tickets, smoked a cigarette, and nursed
a plastic cup of coffee. Rain saturated her freedom — this birth
is anything but. No mother to lick the baby clean. No knock-kneed
moments as baby works to balance. She tore from the rods that held
her in updown motion, kicked her rump high and back, then rocked
back on hind legs to punch the air: her eyes begging for battle.
How she found me is a story for another time, but I can say her head
was always near mine—resistance to law, docility, but how to say she
honors. How to tell you she teaches me to hold on, to bear what
is her greatest kindness. How her sunless birth helped me break,
what it meant to feel the façade of control, and then to gain it,
for a moment. Let me feel, echoed by the roar of her hightail,
she taunts. With love to get on, to learn her body, mine.

Works Cited

Hutchinson-Hall, Dr. John Ellsworth. *Orthodox Saints of the British Isles: Volume III—July—September.* St. Eadfrith Press, 2014.

"Medieval and Ancient Research Centre at the University of Sheffield." *MARCUS*, University of Sheffield, https://sites.google.com/sheffield.ac.uk/marcus/home?authuser=0.

Katherine Gaffney is currently a PhD candidate in Creative Writing at the University of Southern Mississippi, after completing her MFA at the University of Illinois at Urbana-Champaign. Her work has previously appeared or is forthcoming in *jubilat, Rabbit Catastrophe, Harpur Palate, the Mississippi Review, Meridian,* the *Tampa Review*, and elsewhere.

Katherine has received fellowships from the University of Illinois Urbana-Champaign for work on a children's book focusing on the Van Gogh family and the Beatrix Potter Society to attend their annual conference in England. She has also attended the Tin House Summer Workshop and the Juniper Institute for Young Writers Summer Creative Writing Program and been a presenter at the John R. Milton Writer's Conference.

www.ingramcontent.com/pod-product-compliance
Lightning Source LLC
LaVergne TN
LVHW041929090826
845145LV00017B/2768

* 9 7 8 1 6 4 6 6 2 6 9 9 1 *